NOT IN THIS WORLD

Tuesday – Sunday, 11am – 8pm
T +44 (0)20 7921 0943
F +44 (0)20 7921 0607
poetrylibrary.org.uk

Level 5 at Royal Festival Hall
Southbank Centre, Belvedere Road
London SE1 8XX

Books may be renewed by telephone

POETRY LIBRARY
The Saison Poetry Library housing
the Arts Council Poetry Collection at

**SOUTHBANK
CENTRE**

Supported by
**ARTS COUNCIL
ENGLAND**

Tracey Herd was born in Scotland in 1968 and lives in Dundee. She studied at Dundee University, where she was Creative Writing Fellow in 1998-2001. In 1993 she won an Eric Gregory Award, and in 1995 a Scottish Arts Council Bursary.

In 1997 she took part in Bloodaxe's New Blood tour of Britain, and in 1998 was the youngest poet in the British-Russian Poetry Festival organised by the British Council with Bloodaxe when she gave readings in Moscow and Ekaterinburg and her poems appeared on metro trains in Russian cities.

In 2000 she read her poems over the public address system in the winners enclosure at Musselburgh racecourse. In 2002 she collaborated on a short opera, *Descent*, with the composer Gordon McPherson for Paragon Ensemble which was performed at the Traverse Theatre in Glasgow. In 2004 she received a Creative Scotland Bursary.

She was a Royal Literary Fund Fellow at Dundee University in 2009-11. She is now working as a Royal Literary Fund Lector and participating in their Bridge Project.

She has published three collections with Bloodaxe: *No Hiding Place* (1996), which was shortlisted for the Forward Prize for Best First Collection; *Dead Redhead* (2001), a Poetry Book Society Recommendation; and *Not in This World* (2015), a Poetry Book Society Choice shortlisted for the T.S. Eliot Prize.

TRACEY HERD

NOT IN THIS WORLD

BLOODAXE BOOKS

ISBN: 978 1 85224 894 9

First published 2015 by
Bloodaxe Books Ltd,
Eastburn,
South Park,
Hexham,
Northumberland NE46 1BS.

www.bloodaxebooks.com
For further information about Bloodaxe titles
please visit our website or write to
the above address for a catalogue.

Supported using public funding by
**ARTS COUNCIL
ENGLAND**

Cover design: Neil Astley & Pamela Robertson-Pearce.

Printed in Great Britain by Bell & Bain Limited, Glasgow, Scotland, on
acid-free paper sourced from mills with FSC chain of custody certification.

for John

and in memory of Victor Skretkowicz

When life's sun sinks in the west,
Lord, may I have done my best.
May I find sweet peace and rest...

PATSY CLINE (Batiste, Milton)

CONTENTS

We are all sentenced to solitary confinement,
inside our own skins, for life.

TENNESSEE WILLIAMS

Please don't tell, no, no, no
Don't say that I told you so.
I just heard a rumour from a friend.
I don't say that it's true,
I'll just leave that up to you.

BUDDY HOLLY,
'Peggy Sue Got Married'

What I Wanted

was such a plump, bountiful
landscape of snow, more
than I'd ever dared wish for.
That was back when we had
proper winters, long ago,
when lawns and driveways
vanished: there were
no boundaries. Fences, walls,
gardens and homes dropped off
the edge of the world.
There was a muffled
silence each night when
darkness married with snow
to wake me from dreams
that began and ended
with the snow. I was hidden
from view behind a tree
whose branches were
perilously bent and laden
with snow, watching
a dark figure disappear;
then I would slip out fearlessly,
sure-footed and fleet,
with my magnifying glass
and pocket torch to follow
the tracks that led off as far
as a child's eye could see,
and then a little further.

What I Remember

is not the race itself but the evening
which disappeared in a tangle of diving
sunlight and nerves as I hugged myself,
chilled, and waited for the starter, bent
forward, the tang of mown grass
sprayed like water and the white lines
freshly painted on the spongy red track,
breasting the tape, alone and splendid,
queen of my own universe, then the medal
like a tiny sun catching the last of the light,
and feeling as if my heart would burst.

The Little Sister

I was born in America's Midwest:
Nebraska, Kansas, Ohio, a tiny
white frame house with a creaky
old porch where I'd sit

with my baby sister, twisting
the hair of my lumpy old doll
into untidy pigtails; I'd improvise
bleak fairytales, enjoying

her giggling attentions. She died
in a moonlit road accident
when I was ten, blood like rust
running down paintwork. I think

of her often, hoping she didn't suffer,
praying to God in Heaven.
She was pushed in front of a car.
I pray to God for my own salvation.

Not James Dean

Here's a ripped old poster on a crumbling wall
advertising diversions of spectacular dullness; imagine
the tedium of wet afternoons, a bored teen,
not James Dean, hanging around the outskirts
of a dead-end town, unable even to imagine
other afternoons. The grass is a shabby sort of green
and the skeletons of rusting machines
have poisoned the ground. The once gaudy
horses circling the carousel have broken down,
their names peeled, incomplete: Trigger and Champion,
Silver and Blaze, hardly poetry is it? They huddle
miserably in a cold rain, waiting out the decades
for the children who will never come; sometimes
a car door slams and pinch-faced boys
with remote eyes scrabble over the fence,
blowing smoke and oblivious of the weather.

The Fortune Teller

She forecasts catastrophe,
the bread and butter of her psyche.
Wool-gathering is for amateurs.
She won't name names. She can afford
such generosity, she murmurs slyly
as she ushers you into a dingy back room
where the furnishings are eccentric
and the air is thick.

She draws the filthy curtains back:
she used to keep a cat, she tells you
casually, but she had it put to sleep
because it brought her back luck
and scratched her once across the cheek,
missing, by a miracle, one jaundiced eye.
In the cramped back garden nothing grows.
Crows settle briefly on the crumbling wall.
The omens are grim. There are so many of them.

She misquotes *Macbeth* with gloomy relish
running a ragged nail along lines that speak
of witches, massacres, wild-eyed horses. Here, she
looks you unflinchingly in the eye
and predicts a childless future. She can see
a stain that spreads from skin to sheet
and a heavy heart. She can offer neither
amulet nor charm to ward off the demons
lying in wait for us. That, she says,
would be dishonest. She will see you out now.
The dirty hand hovers, palm upwards,
waiting for the expected jangle of silver.

The Living Library

She pushes the reheated food around the plate,
the big brass key rigid in the lock
which she'll go back three times
to check before turning off the radio
and taking the water glass to bed.

Christie, Sayers, Marsh are sitting
well-mannered on the shelf,
pushed in tight to keep
their suave murderers inside,
their victims' choked cries unheard.

She turns over onto her other side,
pushing the pillows forward, back,
thinking of the spinster pulling weeds
and tidying the tubs in her well-tended
garden in St Mary Mead, between murders
as it were, but soon will come
the poison pen, the bullet in the dark
that could have been blindly fired
when the house's lights went out,
but which was only ever meant for one.

The Case of the Inconvenient Corpse

The maid's unnecessarily loud scream
was the first real hint that something
was wrong: that, followed by the sound
of the hot breakfast dishes hitting the floor
and then another scream for good measure.
By this time his wife had dived back
under the covers begging him to go
and see what the matter was. *'Darling, please.'*
Grumbling, he pulled the rich crimson folds
of his dressing-gown tightly around him.

Downstairs, it was worse than he could
have imagined: his favourite room
in the huge, rambling house, sullied, his breakfast
ruined, and the rare Turkish rug, and a broken
French window letting a fresh rain soak
the curtains. It was just too bad.

She would have been pretty without the bloody dent
in her skull, and a little less make-up.
The plummy lipstick had spread halfway across her face
like jam smeared on without a mirror and her roots
were black and lank as river vegetation floating
its tendrils over the dark water. Why couldn't
the bloody river have taken her? Much more
sensible than dragging her here.
He knew he'd never seen her before, although
he knew her type and he'd met plenty like her,
cheap as holiday souvenirs faded by the sun
in some dusty shop window, retaining only patches

of their original colour. Her nails were disgraceful:
a really toxic shade of scarlet where they hadn't been bitten
and chipped and the dirt, dear God, like she'd
been digging with her bare hands in the earth.

Nobody Home

I suppose the mirror told you
I was alive if you can
call this living. You were the last
person that I was expecting.

I wonder whose heart he brought home
and what heroic story he spun.
Did he meet some poor peasant
on the forest track – and wait
until her back was turned – or did he find
something already dead and hack
its heart out, puking everywhere,
thanking God his hands were clean
and his conscience as clear as spring water
as if he hadn't already fucked me over
by leading me into this foul, dark place?

I'll bet he turned as pale as a geisha girl
when the mirror gave us both away.
Ha bloody ha – how did he dig himself
out of that great big hole?

And I don't much care that you're at my door
hammering like a fiend at the wood
with a knife in your hand instead
of the nice juicy apple and seven little men
and my prince dead in your wake.
You're wasting your rancid breath. There's
nobody home. Take a walk across the lawn,
look in the lovely glasshouse. Look

at all the flowers and cards my mourners left
before you so rudely slaughtered them.
And for God's sake, shut up. You're hurting
my head. My dreams are so sweet now.
I think I have earned my eternal rest.

Sheep

God alone knows what's stuck in their throats
although even He is looking elsewhere.
It's as if one of their dishevelled number had swallowed
a car on its patch of gravel and coughed it back up
as the tyres slip and the ancient engine protests.

They nose aimlessly amongst the thin grass
and scatter of rocks on a hillside that ought to be
too steep: somehow, they remain rooted there
like elderly ladies, pleasantly befuddled.
From this distance, they are misshapen dots
that float, detached, from the tired eye.
They look up at nothing and bend their heads
back down against the driving rain.

Vivien and Scarlett

...in Hollywood memory of Vivien was more vivid and dazzling.
To the friends she had there she would always be Scarlett O'Hara.

ANNE EDWARDS: *Vivien Leigh: a Biography*

She read and reread each well-thumbed page
absorbing the part she was born to play,
her green eyes slanting in the fire's feline rage.

Once on deck, she prowled like a beast in its cage
as the fires over old England blazed worlds away.
She read and reread each well-thumbed page.

To her, the world was always a stage.
She was youthful and stubborn, a dreamer and fey,
her green eyes outstaring the fire's wild rage.

Filled with a hunger she could never assuage,
she knelt in Tara's red earth to mourn and to pray
no longer needing to read from the page.

Strange to be fixed as one dazzling image
when her soul was in darkness, losing its way,
her green eyes reflecting the fire's abating rage.

A Southern belle from another war-torn age
for whom tomorrow was always another day
and life held beauty and promise until the lost page
when her green eyes closed on the embers of rage.

Norma Shearer

Norma Shearer had eyes of the palest blue
which photographed almost white
in the wrong kind of light, and really,
her legs were too thick and she knew
that one eye cast about in a delinquent
skew that parodied beauty. She accepted
the unwritten rules, freeing herself
by a rigid adherence: what fun to conform
in portraits by Hurrell, hands cupping
her jaw, all sleek hair and sharp profile
with no one remarkable feature, save for
those eyes of the palest blue. She
impersonated queens and tragic heroines
after going through the rollcall of starlets,
flappers and prettily bobbed poppets,
a meticulous attention to the meanest detail:
sexy suffering in satin gowns, and why not?
After all, you couldn't act.
Play your part and cast it off. Admire your name
in lights above the title. Retire a rich woman,
royalty of sorts.

Sea Birds

The sea is swollen with hurt.
The wind has the sea's grey heart
in its wolfish teeth, pulling
hysterical waves by their
bent, defeated necks towards
an empty beach with its
scattering of huts, rocks
and bladderwrack, slippery
and swollen as a faceful of tears.
It is a perfect seascape

but no one is watching.
The sea is short of breath,
poised briefly then shaken
till the landscape tilts
and the sky is the sea
and the sea is the sky.
The sea birds circle overhead
calling shrilly, goodbye,
goodbye. Goodbye.

Glass House

This is the mansion that God willed me
and no other. The ceiling is glass,
the sky unreadable and what pass
for stars stare blankly

at something just over my shoulder.
I am standing in the grand hall of mirrors
like a chess piece on the tiled floor,
a blind and insignificant player in a game

that the other has already won,
but I am trapped on my square while you
are making love to another who is
shivering but not with the cold,

and I am laid bare against the world.

Hall of Mirrors

His gallery was a hall of mirrors.
I floated its length like a lone black swan,
its half-open eyes taking nothing in
for blank was my image in his mirror.

Each day I died, stripping my flesh from bone,
begging his skilful hands to make me come
alive again. I wanted him to take me home
but he betrayed me with my silent twin.

I was his graceless, heartless mannequin
lovingly gifted into another.
He gave her lips in warm, breathing colour.
When the paint had dried he touched her skin.

Eyes Wide Shut

'It wouldn't take much for it to happen,' you say
deliberately, and I am left behind, a failed actress,
holding the script – which is in tatters –
and my private screening of what
my head has rejected, till now,
when the music booms into the packed auditorium
where the audience eagerly await
my humiliation, as I sit, unable to move,
as the picture unfolds, bit by bit
and the soundtrack kicks in.
Your bare chest is poised above
her breasts, her legs are spread, her head
thrown back. Her arms are around you,
shutting me out. You gaze at her open mouth
and shout her name as you come
and I mouth your name as she screams
it on the screen and I can't close my eyes.
I can't piece my heart back into a life but I rock
quietly forward, back, with my arms wrapped
around myself as you and she begin again
to make love and the curtain closes
on your little world.

The Diner

I took a bullet for you
last night, but it wasn't real.
Nothing is real, absolutely nothing.
Absolute is a fantasy. Absolution
a helpless prayer, unanswered.
Not even your indifference bothered me
as the bullet I couldn't quite believe in
tore through me, coins clattering
in the jukebox, records falling,
a harsh breath before the music.

I touched the entry wound. It was dry.
Something coppery and red gleamed
star-like on the floor, rolling exuberantly,
a playful, yet ghostly child.
I could see through everyone.

You sipped coffee
and didn't even look up.
It should have hurt. I tried
to make it hurt but I
didn't have the heart. I should
have put you in your place,
at your scuffed table, the cracked
tiles in my head. We weren't even
in the same dream. I am wise
to you now. I won't take another
bullet for you. But I will.
I won't. I will. Lie still,
you said from a distant universe

where I was tearing at the petals
of flesh and watching coldly
as they fell. He loves me. He loves
me not. Lie still. This isn't real.
The last words are mine. I won't,
I will, I won't, I will.

You Can't Take My World from Me

Why did you give no warning? You got up to go
and left me here with the music, alone.
No please, I really don't want to know.

Doors slam. I have locked every window.
My heart echoes in an empty mansion
asking over and over, why did you go?

Well, you can't take my world with you.
I have decided to turn my heart into stone
because I really don't ever desire to know.

The lilies bloom; those skies, the sun's glow:
I have chiselled my final question
on the tiny white stone. Why did you go?

The sunset is beautiful, the darkness slow,
oh I have cut myself to the very bone
and I simply don't want to know.

I've left you now with the script you'll follow
so you will never forget what you've done.
You will never black out your decision to go.

And as for the reason, I will never know.

When a Lovely Flame Dies

When your heart's on fire, you must be alive

Snow thickens like a muffled melody:
silently, on the wooden stage, the encore dies
as the tail-lights slip quietly down the sky.

The mangled wreckage will always lie
against that fence, snow flurrying as the plane taxis.
Stars beckon. The snow plays its muffled melody

and the ghostly lovers will never rise. They lie
in the snow, peaceful in their shattered bodies
after the tail-lights have slid quietly down the sky.

During the last black acres and hours of ice
each heart has played out its final goodbye.
The snow chokes on its muffled melody

blanketing the memories which it crystallises
into glass and ice. No more tears, no more lies
after the tail lights had slipped quietly down the sky:

Flakes of snow then, drifting down like a blessing, a cry
although only fools believe in an unearthly paradise.
The snow wipes out every treacherous memory.
The tail-lights disappeared like red stars from the sky.

At the Captain's Table

The once pristine white cloth,
oceans of linen with its food stains
and discarded napkins, twisted:
the crystal glasses of champagne,
the golden liquid gone,
old toasts forgotten,
including your silent one.
For you, he left the lights blazing.

The others are all in bed.
They left before you,
years ago. Their hands are so cold.
Their hearts are stopped.
No one will rewind the clocks.
She examines her own hands,
the lifeline she'd outlived,
faint as the flickering
wrecker's lights at her wrists,
beckoning her onto the rocks
beside the smashed up ships.
In her hand she rests her head
and all its confused decades,
the losing hand she played.

For seconds, she thought
she was twenty again,
blonde and dancing
with an uncommon grace,
until the mirror spat
its cruel portrait back in her face.

She remembers how he flinched away
as she went to kiss him on the cheek,
as daylight rendered her physical,
as if he'd just seen her for the first time.
That was the last time.
Each night, your bed is empty.
The lovers are entangled next door.
Isn't it terribly lonely?

Your life is a series of port-holes
each with its precious, tiny view.
Turn the mirror to the wall.
Open one more bottle
if you can stagger to the bar.
Watch the pulses leap like shipwrecks.
You are covered in veins,
like a map, blue and green on white.
It isn't pretty. You couldn't read it
to save yourself, even if you wanted to.

When you undress, you'll cry
without thinking.
The party's over and it's time.
Roll up the charts.
The ship has set its course.
It won't ride out the storm.
The Captain is on the bridge,
empty eye-sockets looking out
at the emptiness of the sea.
His bony fingers turn the wheel
into the rotting teeth of the gale.
How many ships have run aground
on the rocks in the dark and storms.
Who's counting? Who really cares?

Vessel

the hands of the clock are folded as in prayer

JILES PERRY RICHARDSON (THE BIG BOPPER)

Never return to that which you once loved, even on
a blazing July afternoon, when dubious memories will
overwhelm you like bubbles of champagne, and the world
seems childlike and full of possibilities again.
You'll negotiate the overgrown track, only to find
a burned-out shell, a derelict heart, the silence of long gone
gangs of children, although behind a blackened tree,
you'll think you hear a little boy, invisible, his giggles
barely audible. Don't reach out. Turn away.

You carefully turn over the soil under the trees where
the cherished past lies: a richly decorated vase,
gold-rimmed with sunshine and alive with flowers:
red and yellow, your favourite colours. It was wrapped in cloth
in a weatherproof box in a hidden corner you thought
was your secret childhood place. You were wrong.

You pull out mere fragments that will cut each eager
finger down to the bone, and if by some sharp twist
of fate each piece is found and glued together,
the picture will be darker. A sunset will have
become a storm; roses and lilies, soulless monochrome;
and the completed vessel won't hold water. As you sit
in the darkness, your illusions shattered, you
will realise that nothing stays secret forever
and that midnight is the only memory which
gives up the key to open the old, stiff lock.
But turn away from the door. Don't look up at the clock.

The Imaginary Death of Star

Her heart cracks like a figurine,
a skater holding one skate,
frozen in her final spin.

She is clutching the blade,
not the blunt part, deliberately:
her heart and palm bleed.

Her white costume glitters
with its thousand sequins
before the tiny mirrors shatter,

faces shooting into the night.
He is watching beside the ice
as she breaks in the spotlight.

The audience throw roses
onto the ice, soft toys, applause.
Her body lies in its awkward pose.

His reaction is to stare
coldly at the broken thing.
The rink is covered in bloody litter.

He walks in the almost black.
The moon is motionless above the frost.
She is gone. She won't come back.

He has a red petal on his sole
shimmering in the cold.
He grinds it carelessly until

frost and petal are one,
scarlet shreds and sparkling crystals.
Sometimes, he enjoys being alone.

He looks up to the sky:
her name was Star, that slutty tattoo.
He wipes the sharp blade dry.

At other times he needs
a chorus line of trashy girls.
To make their soft throats bleed.

Archive

Red brick and ivy in shadow and sun:
the sun makes crude annotations on stone
as I shelter in the shadows' margin,

reluctant to open the heavy oak door
and climb the worn, unfamiliar stairs
to an attic library where the sweltering air

is thick with disruptions. Every paper-
stuffed box hoards invisible mysteries
of skin, sloughed off from each interloper.

Now which is you and what is other?
The patterns of ink on each paper are
Rorschach blots of artful disorder.

I remember a spider in amber, the bubbles
of air as if it breathed still in its jewel
world, the inclusions of plant and animal

matter, the past, scattered and miniature,
lifted from the primeval forest floor.
It passed from one hand to another.

Joan Fontaine and Rebecca

You were never given a name of your own. The dead had a name,
Rebecca, and the sad lunatic down at the shack by the shore.
Even that damned house had a name: Manderley,
when you broke the porcelain figurine, I thought it was a portent
of things to come. I thought your fragile mind would shatter.
You were always huddled against the world, all nervous, flitting
        gestures.
Handing out the scripts, Hitchcock casually let slip that the cast and
        crew
hated you. Olivier had no time for you. He wanted his Scarlett,
        black-haired
with eyes the colour of a dangerous green sea. He wanted to drown.
Her dark hair blowing in the wind...
You walked into the West Wing with its view of the sea. Danvers
        followed silently
to present Rebecca's wardrobe of fine, expensive things, lingerie she
        held onto a little too long,
a monogrammed pillow slip, the nightgown by the immaculately
        turned down bed as if each dawn
Rebecca would return from the tour of her domain and slip silently
        into her gown. *Have you ever*
seen anything so delicate? Clumsily you turned and ran from the room
        but you returned.
In Rebecca's cursed final masquerade costume, you leaned out into
        the misty night,
Mrs Danvers perched like an angel of death at your china white,
        flawless shoulder
whispering as if from far far away, out at sea, luring the tiny vessel
        onto the rocks.

Rebecca echoes her entreaties from the ocean floor, coughing up
 rocks and shells.
She is possessed by Rebecca, her memory sailing at the edge of
 reason. Would you
have jumped had the warning flares not shot up? I like to think not.
 You were
the only one of them with any sense. *She can't speak. She can't bear
 witness.*
She can't harm you any more. But nobody bothered to listen. Ship of
 fools.
In the end, it wasn't quite the burning of Atlanta, but Manderley
 put on
quite a show, brutal against the dark skies, a false dawn and Mrs
 Danvers
dancing dementedly like Rebecca's puppet for the last time, running
from window to window. And you, walking placidly with Rebecca's
 dog
over the lawn in front of a burning skeleton. In the end, fragile girl
 with no name,
whose father painted the same tree for eternity, you survived them
 all.

Olivia de Havilland

Dr. When am I most real?

VIRGINIA STUART CUNNINGHAM, *The Snake Pit*

Atlanta burned down months before you fled the scene,
safely captured on celluloid, the city façade that never was.
You were half dead from giving birth. Strange how both sisters fled
the flames in their most famous films and how Melanie loved Scarlett
like a sister. Rhett told Scarlett harshly: *She loves you, let that be your*
    curse.
In the back of the wagon you showed tenderness, not fear as you
    reached out weak arms
for the son who almost killed you. Then the pain. You couldn't even
    twist
your gold wedding band for comfort as you'd given it away for the
    cause.
You had so little left but courage. You were the only one of the four
    leads
who died on screen. Now you have outlived them all by decades, your
    quiet strength
you were the only actress who wanted Melanie, seeing in her qualities
most were blind to. *I loved her so. Melanie was... a caring person.*
A good woman but also an intelligent woman and a tough woman.
Most of all she was a ...woman with a great capacity for happiness.

Perhaps, in the world of the screen, you connect with your sister
or do you simply not bother to watch each other?
Do certain lines make you cry or smile?
'There's a naturally strong rivalry between sisters' (*Dark Mirror*).
Two twins, one good, the other evil. You played them both. So who
    was real:

the nervous, loving one, or the knife-wielding lunatic who played a
    symphony
on her sister's nerves? The good twin believed her sister innocent.
She started jumping at shadows, swallowing sleeping pills then waking
    at the brief,
bright light which swept the bedroom and then was gone when she
    awoke.
But it was The Snake Pit where I think you almost touched, in the
    asylum
where you cast off your name, your husband and your own beauty.
Zipped up to the chin in the ice bath, you had visions of the stormy
waters off Manderley. But only briefly. I wanted to create a rose,
a hybrid to bring you both together. But that would be too elaborate.
You were both blue girls with golden hope, apart. I picked your flower,
The name almost an afterthought. Forget-me-not.

Brigadoon

In 2011, a Vegas tycoon left $4 million to the National Trust
for Scotland before committing suicide. Although he had never
visited Scotland he had loved his fantasies of a long vanished
land. His mythical Scotland was most famously portrayed in
Brigadoon where the American traveller, Tommy, meets and falls
in love with the mysterious Fiona.

Far better if he'd said farewell forever and returned
to his American bitch, her withering elegance, the bars
all mirrors and champagne, each airy bubble far more
substantial than Brigadoon. She was a dream of foaming
primrose skirts, dancing foot-perfect through forests
of white heather, but memory would have taken care
of her. Far better these New York streets with
their chipped stone exteriors drenched with weather
than the phantom country rising from the mists,
once every blessed century, removed from history.
Only the arching bridge seemed real, stone on stone.
He turned his back on the village and crossed back over.

Mid-century, he retired to the gritty glare of the Vegas desert,
a recluse who'd shaken hands with Eisenhower. Fifty years
later he wrote his will in a firm, determined hand leaving
millions to the memory of bonnie lassies who breathed
like rain-soaked breezes only in the soundstage of his mind.
He fired a bullet through his brain. The scenery cracked.
Did he leave believing his dark journey would
carry him over desert, cities, a chilly ocean, or had he
accepted that night cannot shape the welcoming
silhouettes of inns and houses, spark them into life and light.
The stars are clearer in the desert than almost anywhere.
In his fine house he lies. His heart still bleeds for her.

Louise Brooks

Pearls strung around a neck
of marble, lustrous beads
hard and pretty: the hair is black,
the lips rubescent. Ghost men feed

on these painted curves, define
a role you played with vigour, silent
vigour. The eyes are cool and sane.
The mood is violent.

Dreams of Lost Summers and Found Lines

'Grandma will take us rowing on the lake,'
you texted me, and I was fooled into thinking
it real. As if you were still a little girl.
It won't ever happen. You passed
each other briefly, six weeks on this earth
together. She is sixteen summers away.

When was the last time we took the rowboat out?
Last century? All these missing years. It was
a scorching summer: we were all burned,
sprawled on the grass by the water's edge
awaiting our half-lifetime on the water.

Sometimes I smell roses in her bedroom
or parma violets, when I'm drifting off.
She spent her last years in this bed, reading
old green and cream Penguin novels,
addicted to her detective stories. In the evening
she enjoyed a small sherry. If only the dark amber
liquid could have better preserved the memories.

Now, lying quietly beneath an oak tree, does
she hear the little blonde girl, grown up now,
playing her viola, the sweet, note-perfect recital
floating through the warm, summer air,
always a dreamer, a part of her music?

There is a land of the living and a land of the dead and the bridge is love, the only survival, the only meaning.

THORNTON WILDER

Leaving

The cherry blossoms are wild. It's May
and the sky is fresh, a lively grey.

The tree is blown by gusts of light;
for now, the exuberant flowers hold tight.

Flushed, they tease the wind, dancing
girls waltzing out their spring.

Spring was far too short:
the briefest charm and flirt

but there are no obvious omens of loss,
just a renegade cloud fired across

the bow of a ship sailing out into evening.
Somewhere, someone much loved is leaving.

Reverie

This little moon, this disintegrating pearl,
this snowflake on my tongue;
I will pull the curtains tightly shut,
and the mirror is the real sky where light
has travelled from another galaxy,
from you to me, and I can half make out
your face in the smudged glass, smudged
as if our fingers had tried to touch, where
we might waltz silently away from here.
I haven't slept for days but the invitation
was too beautifully worded to refuse,
engraved in gold on white vellum, no name.
It lies on the table by my bed, invisible.

At first, the chandeliers blaze and my steps
are dizzily graceful, then the light begins
to blur and you are far from me.
Darkness steps in and I have a new partner
who leads me from the polished floor,
up one thousand spiral stairs, stripping
the ballgown from my shoulders and hanging
up the day with all the other lacerating days.
I step out from the constriction of memory,
its rigid seams, the red welts digging
into my skin. I am raw and naked,
released. My breathing starts to slow.
It is a balancing act, this. I think my feet bleed.

Glass slippers were never made for dancing,
and one is always lost by the careless
ghost of the crying girl, pulled back

into her past, wrists bruised. I think
tiny jewels are falling from my flesh,
loosened by each loosening breath.
Now I am unadorned. I can't feel anything.
I am drifting and the music is receding,
so far away. The candles are blown out.
You have left my heart, thank God,
the bullet retrieved, a dull clatter on the floor,
another scar but no more blood.
I live for these blank, black hours, when
I no longer have to count the stars,
tracing shapes in the sky, a face
that was there all too briefly. Oblivion.

For a few hours I have left life's
masquerade, but one day when the door
of the mansion slams behind me,
I will finally be by myself. It is so easy
to push people away with words twisted
like the roots of trees, while the heart
mouths, silently, only to itself
in the forest, yards from the wolves:
it is cold and dark outside. Don't
leave me here. Please.

No Reason

I kneel in the snow, hands bare.
Everything is black and white here
like a still from an old film:
the darkness of the sky, soaked denim,
the backdrop of the twisted trees.
Cars pass with the murmur of hearts.
Their headlights almost blind me.
Tonight, it is cloudless and chilled.
Your letters are white. The paper
is unnaturally bright under the light
of millions of opals. The snow
shines like an opal, fierce flashes
of colour. There is an Arab legend
that opals are lightning strikes
which hit earth and the white stones
can't quite contain their lightning.
There's also a legend that when
the owner dies, the stone loses
all colour. Lilies are propped
against your grave which simply
has your name, lifespan, *beloved*...
the words rolling like endless credits.
You are more alive in your letters.
I wrote a short poem for your grave
but I have no practical tools
and no right to desecrate
your family's special place.
I map the stars, night after night,
hoping to find *your star in heaven*
but I don't believe there is anything

after this life, so it is a quest
without rhyme nor reason.
You are no ghost, nor are you lost.
You have simply left forever.
We will not meet *in a better place*,
nor will we ever be again together.

Sometimes, I think I hear my name,
as if through the breeze, a whisper.
Not you, just a wicked trick of the restless
wind, but it is moments like that
that I live for.

Cemetery in Snow

Mausoleum of snow I have built for you,
my frozen hands sifting the drifts,
plunging into the glaring flakes.
I might be inside a snow globe, a child's delight.
My world has shrunk to this midnight scene.
My memories have almost gone. It is winter
forever. I will never leave: the rusted gates are iced shut.

I am haloed by the blue-lit flakes. Angel wings
brush my skin. I have frozen angel dust on my tongue.
Yes, I might be a child again, the furies of snow
stinging my eyes. I was dumb when I came here.
Now all I can see is the snow and all sounds
are muffled as if I held mittened hands over
my ears although my head and ears are bare.
Somewhere, I think, someone has lit a fire.
The warmth comes from another world entirely.
Hold my hand, friend. We will not be lonely.

Happy Birthday

It would have been your birthday today.
The Furies found me and brought me
a cake and lit the candles with their fiery
breath. The heat is intolerable. Perhaps
this is what it is like to be in Hell.
You'll never blow them out. I didn't
allow you even one breath. Their eyes
are dripping blood as I did. The nurses
told me to keep my eyes shut. Well,
you were just a random selection of cells,
nothing like me at all. I still wanted
to see you, my little bloody paperweight.
Could I have counted your toes and fingers,
seen ancestors in your tiny face? The drugs
made me float like a sunset above my aching
body. *By the 22nd week the eyes have formed*
but the irises still lack pigment and are shut.

Every month, I lie like a broken mannequin
on the bed. There is a fist or a heart
in my stomach and the furies are here
to remind me I am empty, although
there's no need. I know why I bleed.
You were scraped away like unwanted food.
Look at you lying there in your little glass coffin,
or is it a snow globe? Were you terribly cold?
Will I sprinkle your cradle with snow? Will
you wake in one hundred years and see
my face in the mirror and shudder?
Will the trees have grown up to the skies,

the briars and roses climbing your stone wall,
the Prince circling on his white horse,
the rope pulling tighter? He will never
have any intention of rescuing you,
in your bloody shift with your blind eyes.

Solo

On the icy lake
she sits, skirts
a rime-scrolled
lily. The moon
spotlights her
little circle,
her head is bowed.

Roses bloom
from her wrists,
scarlet
corsages she
fashioned herself
from flesh and vein.
She is here again,
holding an empty
gilt frame.

There is a frozen
audience of trees,
rocks, and endless snow.
This is how it goes.

She is both the black
swan and the white,
depending upon
the shifting light.
Her corps de ballet
has taken flight,
these feathered girls

in pristine white
illuminate some
other night.

She waits
for a decade, or
half a century.
The ice will disintegrate.
Greedily, she will
breathe water,
sinking into epitaph.
She has a gravestone
in her head. She is
already dead.

The ice will reform.
A final prayer,
hands clasped together,
as if to an invisible other.
Hope was always
the hunter's arrow.
It will be as if
she had never lived:
a girl with nothing
left to give.

The Afternoon Shift Are Leaving
the Port Talbot Steelworks

The men are leaving the Port Talbot Steelworks
as the day is sharpening its edge on a bright sky.
They stream through the last-ever light in the world,
their tread, heavy and tired, but their heads unbowed
as they set their soft caps at the afternoon. Their
faces are blurred because they are just a little too far
from where the man with the camera stands.
A few steps forward would have sharpened the focus
but it is better to be uncertain. They are merely
a group of anonymous men. No one is marked.
It will always be afternoon and a brilliant one
where grubby sleeves are rolled to the elbows
to catch the sun, and where the men walk forward
towards the children, the unborn and the never
to be born. Somewhere, the photographer
has caught the shadow of a shadow.

A copper penny bearing the King's silhouette
is found by a little boy under the kerb where
it rolled after wobbling like an old bicycle
over the stones. A copper penny for every
last thought. Steel reflects the sun all over
Europe and the Pacific. The machines don't
stop, night or day, although, one by one,
the anonymous men are slipping away.

Momentum

The dark brown colt gallops briskly resolute,
sanguine, one certain length away from victory,
his exuberant rider standing almost straight up
in the irons, grinning face turned to the camera,
whip flung in triumph above his head,
whooping with youthful brazenness, reins
pulled tight but no matter because no earthly
force could stall this horse, which came from
last to first in ground-devouring strides,
carried wide but well balanced, unsurprised
by his own smooth acceleration.
Now he is deaf to the crowds' sharp inhalation,
their involuntary response to the boy's unbridled
and audacious joy before he'd even passed
the necessary winning-post, the legend cast
in a split green second before the shutter's click,
the confirmation, the camera's sharp, impartial
eye conferring victory by a mere brown head.

Ruffian

When Ruffian was first displayed for public consideration on May 22, 1974 her purpose on earth quickly became apparent... to reveal, once and for all, how big, how beautiful, and how fast a thoroughbred racehorse could be, and how the combination could be deadly when taken to Ruffian's physical extremes.

Champion: the lives, times and past performances of America's greatest thoroughbreds (2005)

They call it *the look of eagles*, that gaze beyond the skies.
You were marked from the start with your white star
and the band just above your left hind foot
with three dots, one for each year on this earth.
You were drawn and shaded in with charcoal
but it is unlucky to call a racehorse 'black'.
On your gravestone you are dark brown or bay.

This is not how you were supposed to go or when
although all you knew was how to run
and even when your leg had snapped, you ran
and ran and ran, your heart stronger than the fractured
limb which splintered like wood in the Belmont dirt,
Your jockey simply couldn't pull you up although, God, he tried.
If any horse could have outrun death, my money
would have been on your dark head and you eyeballed
each other for a stretch, Foolish Pleasure running far ahead
in a race that would never really count.

You were buried close to where you finally stumbled to a halt,
your ebony nose pointed towards the finish line
in the infield at Belmont Park. You would never leave the track.
The evening turned as dark as your coat. As champions are,
you were buried whole, a huge, white shrouded mangled thing

where once a living horse had been, one who could outrun almost
everything. No horse on earth could live with you, even from the
    first
few strides: every race run from the front, wire to wire.

A solitary red rose for inside your grave. It fell beside your head
before the ground filled up with soil again and the lawn looked
    pristine.
It covered the white-shrouded beauty, still wearing her red,
embroidered blankets, perfectly smoothed. It still mattered
that you were immaculately turned out under the floodlights
for the final time. No one wanted to leave you, alone. Farewell,
    fierce girl.

Spring in the Valley of the Racehorse

In her well-tended garden,
March is always a revelation, a generous
parcelling-out of leaf
and feather, the branches
sieving dark green onto pale
and the small birds fluent.

An untried colt, he ran green,
tilting awkwardly at the windmills
of spring that swung the shadows
and the sun around
in dizzying beats
upon the firm ground.
Still, he ran out an easy winner,
unbothered by the coppery
heat of the afternoon.

She shines the window-glass;
her cloth, a starter's
old-fashioned flag. The breeze
is brisk, her pace easy.
She is well within herself.
The fine weather holds.
Any cloudbursts will be light
and temporary.

He tenses against the hot
metal of the starting-gate
eyeballing the wide swatch
of flat green that vanishes
sweetly into the distance.

He's learned to ignore
the impure source of noise,
the sharp, irregular
flashes of the sun
on glass discs, to keep
his mind within
the miraging posts of white,
evenly spaced along the track.
He blows a little, focused
as the noonday sun
that would blind a person
were they to look at it too long
and too hard.

Near Clearlake, Idaho

In the drifting, swirling snow,
the ground above, the sky below,
this is where God made you disappear
from all earthly radar.
'We belong together for all eternity.'
'This'll be the day we say goodbye.
This'll be the day we die.'
'Honey, that clock looks so lonely
as the tear runs down its face.'
But let's find a better memory
of Chantilly lace and a pretty face,
and a pony-tail hanging down.
'Oh baby, you know what I like!'

Five Seconds

Funny how five seconds...never mind,
enough to remember that perfectly
ordinary coin, pulled, still warm
from Allsop's pocket, the hoarse
command to 'call!', a quarter
flipped into the freezing air
as both men puffed clouds of steam,
and rubbed cold hands together.
How could you have known,
as the coin spun that you were
flipping between life and death,
death and life, life and death?
One man had to lose. The coin
fell and you both bent down.
The stories differ, but I think
it was heads, so Ritchie went
to retrieve his overnight bag
from the freezing coach,
marvelling at his good luck.

Whilst Clearlake sleeps,
one man paces his room,
convinced that he watched
the tail-lights of his Beechwater
Bonanza dip then disappear.

It was simply his imagination,
his companion said, but he knew.
He will phone Fargo, North Dakota
many times that snow-choked night
to see if they'd checked in. They

will never check in. They lie
broken in the snow, soft flurries
drifting over their bodies, curtains
of snow but no last encore.
The Big Bopper sang of having no coat
for his back or no shoes for his feet.
The crash which flung him over
forty feet and a fence tore the clothes
from his body. The angels must have
had the night off although he swore that
someone's watching over you tonight.
He'll watch you as you rest your head.
To Buddy it really doesn't matter any more
but rave on anyway if you can.
Ritchie, only seventeen, impatient,
C'mon let's go.

The Music Men

Out into the dark, star-laden night,
the snow piling up like gambling chips
all over the state. Was God licking
His lips? Here, the weather is freezing
but no snow as yet, just frost and chill.
At one o'clock on February 3rd, a small
Beechwater Bonanza takes off from
Mason City, Iowa. It doesn't have
very far to go, but nobody knows
that God has orchestrated wind shear
and a horizontal snow for just after
take-off. The warning from the tower
goes unheard. A wing scrapes snow
from the roof of a house and spins
as God shakes the world or just
an isolated cornfield in Iowa.
You wouldn't have known much
beyond the snow as the plane
crumples into a fence, like paper.
How many songs were lost
as four men turned to ghosts?
There was a show called *The Music Men*
playing nearby. You just dropped in.

The following morning, acres of snow
and curtains pulled back. He takes
a plane along the same route
as last night and sees something
in a field that his co-pilot swears blind
is a hog house. They land, the night winds
still howling tunelessly. There will be

no new stars in the sky. This is
the graveyard of broken men where
they will always remain, amidst
each winter's tumble of snow, beside
the metal guitar and inscribed silver discs,
Buddy's horn-rimmed glasses. Doctor
T.J. Eckleburg looks over a different
landscape of isolation in more sober
frames. Yet the end result is the same,
that pilgrimage back into the past.

Not Fade Away

In an overgrown cemetery, slipping downhill,
an impossibly steep hill, held in place
by a low wall, the views of the canal
running its clogged-up artery through the village,
I walk through darkness even though
it is mid-afternoon. The stumpy trees
cling to each other, the graves slant
awkwardly like drunks. Here nothing
speaks or creaks or rustles. It is like
being in a silent film, black and white,
distorted by the dark green light
that comes from I can't tell where.
You spoke often of being with the angels
but I can't believe in the incorporeal.
The only angel is sad-faced with scarred
limbs, looking down as if heaven were mud
at her feet. She is petrified, her head bowed,
her hands wrung stonily together in prayer
as if God had struck her with a lightning flash
after promising her the earth, pretending
that this included the leaving of it. Sick,

that sharp sting that brings me face to face
with you, as if my veins briefly brought us back
to life, back to memory which was not how
it was supposed to be. The trees are closer
than ever as if they had grown for a century
and never been pruned back. Have we been
sleeping for one hundred years? Faces float
like moons: Mae Marsh, the girl with the bee stung lips,
bee sting, gentle bee sting, blonde, beautiful, bee stung.

Now the afternoon light is a shining halo of blonde
then as the sun slips down the chorus line,
Clara Bow, flaming youth personified,
all auburn hair and scarlet smile bursts out
dancing her frantic Charleston.

Night and we are alone. I touch her chipped neck,
her verdigris eyelids, her weatherbeaten hands,
her broken wings, wings of marble. She
can barely tolerate their weight. I
almost think she will speak to me for
I have shown her kindness, but her lips
are closed forever and underneath the stiff
white shift, her heart is broken.
The gates of what could have been
a low budget Heaven are rusted shut,
browning flowers entwined and crumbling.
The script is scattered. The stars are dead.
I feel a rush of rain, then nothing. My lids
are too heavy to open. My back is bowed
and my hands won't move. My face
is an ugly cracked blankness.

The Unicorn Seat

(for Elsie and Lucy who once had such a magical place)

The night is warm and we walk down
the winding track, under a green-lit
tunnel of trees. I have one little hand

in each of mine and you both stare up
at the arching evening. The fantastical
birds swoop down, flashing their magical

plumage, outstretching wings of scarlet,
azure, gold and green. They are our guardians.
They will watch over two girls and a woman

making their way to the small, battered seat
with their unicorn, led by its silken halter
which, tonight, is mauve,

the colour of storms when the worst
has passed and the light is reasserting itself.
We stop by the bench and I wipe rainwater

from the slats. You untie our gentle companion.
Don't worry, you tell me. *She never strays very far
and she always comes back to us.*

Just One Request

This is your favourite place on earth
which you are about to leave, walking
slowly out into the waters of the Mar de Plata,
the malignancy blooming for a second time
without cease, as unstoppable as spring.
It was your decision, your body violated
enough. You will leave this world whole.
No one will slice through skin and tissue,
shrinking muscle, for what's the point
in tearing you open when the flower's
roots are everywhere, their gnarled fingers
clutching at your heart. The waves are moving
towards the shore. You are walking away.
There is a dignity in knowing when to leave,
pushing back your chair from the glittering table
with its candles and cut crystal glasses,
quietly excusing yourself, picking up your coat
and walking out into the uncertainty of night.
There is a time for departure even when
there's no certain place to go. Your name
means struggle, noble, ready for battle.
I throw a single white flower on the waters.
Don't think for one minute that it signifies
surrender. I know that you wouldn't care
and love you for it all the more.

Calling Card

(i.m. Marina Keegan, 1989-2012)

At the last party,
the punctual, the late arrivals,
the ones who never made it
are all one and the same.

Girl in the vivid, yellow peacoat,
with hands tucked into your sleeves,
bangles upon bangles; only
in a photograph, could you be silent.

Your life comprised 8,252 sunrises
and one less sunset.
You are at the top of your
radio tower, speaking
out into the universe.
Your words, considered and private
will travel outwards forever
...*thoughts that wander*
through eternity...

The car hit the guard rail,
Dennis, Mass, on Route 6,
with your boyfriend asleep at the wheel,
prosaic details you'd have discarded.
They meant nothing, just
a mess of metal and broken glass.
Your words couldn't protect you,
but they never left you,
swirling around your body like moths.

It's us they'll haunt, bearing
their bright, yellow buds.
I'll never be able to look at
a yellow rose again
without thinking of you.

Your ashes were scattered
against the wind, your body
burned into charred scraps
of paper, random phrases,
all we are in the end.
But you, you were rare. Your words
are up there with the stars,
still travelling outwards
with the occasional earthbound sigh.

ACKNOWLEDGEMENTS

Acknowledgements are due to the editors of the following publications some of these poems first appeared: *The Atlanta Review* (USA), *The Best Scottish Poems 2010 chosen by Jen Hadfield* (Scottish Poetry Library), *Double Bill*, ed. Andy Jackson (Red Squirrel Press, 2014), *Identity Parade: New British & Irish Poets*, ed. Roddy Lumsden (Bloodaxe Books, 2010), *Ploughshares* (USA), *Poetry International* (US), *Poetry International Web*, *The Scotsman*, and *Split Screen*, ed. Andy Jackson (Red Squirrel Press, 2012).

I would like to thank Bloodaxe and my remarkably patient and supportive editor, Neil Astley. This book would not have seen the light of day without his encouragement. I would also like to thank Creative Scotland (then the Scottish Arts Council) for their award of a writer's bursary in 2004. The late Gavin Wallace was especially supportive. The Royal Literary Fund have shown faith in me when I wasn't writing much and I would like to thank all my colleagues there, especially Steve Cook and David Swinburne. Many thanks go to my dear friends John and Isobel Haldane for the use of their kitchen table during the early hours and the peaceful atmosphere in which I wrote so much of this book. Andrew Jackson commissioned poems for his popular culture anthologies which helped ease me back into writing. Again, thank you. Thanks also go to my husband Dave for his continuing support and suggestions; Tim Kearns, Head of English at Kilgraston Girls' School; Stephen Lucas and Ian Mailer for reading drafts of the manuscript; Elsie and Lucy for simply being Elsie and Lucy; Ilyse Kusnetz for her transatlantic support and valued friendship; and Elspeth Cook for reminding me of the early days. If I've missed anyone out, my apologies. Your help was still much appreciated.

Finally I have to say thank you to the late actress Elizabeth Hartman who was by my side all though the writing of *Not in This World*. Which was only fair as she stirred up the word pot again.